Reprinted from the edition of 1939, New York
First AMS EDITION published 1970
Manufactured in the United States of America

International Standard Book Number: 0-404-02949-3

Library of Congress Catalog Card Number: 70-131508

AMS PRESS, INC.
NEW YORK, N.Y. 10003

THE
ARMENIAN CHURCH

BY

PAPKEN CATHOLICOS GULESSERIAN

TRANSLATED BY
TERENIG VARTABED POLADIAN

SECOND EDITION

AMS PRESS, INC.
NEW YORK

INTRODUCTION

The present little volume was written by one of the most eminent scholars of the Armenian Church, Papken I., Catholicos of the Armenians of Cilicia. The book was published in 1936 in the French and Arabic languages.

The author has dedicated this book "To all those who desire to have a clear and complete idea of the Armenian Church, her history, her dogmas, and her rites."* The last chapter deals with the social and economic problems of Armenians in Syria and Lebanon. We have not translated this last chapter because it does not have great interest for the Armenians in America.

This work, although small, has great value, because it is not written by one from without but by one from within. He is a distinguished Catholicos, the supreme head of the Armenian Church. He puts forth merely the facts and beliefs of his own church. He does not sacrifice the truth for the sake of religious controversies. He writes with an independence of doctrinal view points which is so well portrayed in his preface.

Our aim in translating this volume is threefold:

1. To place before the English speaking people

* Page 5.

who are interested in ecclesiastical history, an authentic, brief account of The Armenian Church.

2. To dispel the prevailing misapprehensions and misrepresentations about The Church of Armenia current even in Theological Schools and Seminaries.

3. And, chiefly, to give to the young English speaking generation of Armenians in America a precise knowledge of their church, which has been for twenty centuries the "Torch bearer" of Christianity in the East.

The author has not made any attempt to write a full history of the Armenian Church. It would have been an enormous task to have written a full one and would not attract the attention of the ordinary reader. His purpose, as we want to emphasize again, is to give the most striking incidents which give a clear insight into The Oldest National Church in Christendom.

For fuller information, about our Church, I suggest to my readers "The Church of Armenia" written by one of the most famous authorities of the Armenian Church, Archbishop Malachia Ormanian, former patriarch of Constantinople, published in London 1912, by A. R. Mowbray and Co., Ltd.

We believe that this new book will arouse in the minds of the Armenian youth a deep love and a true appreciation of their church. It will also develop for Protestant Episcopal Churchmen a keener sympathy with a stronger confidence in The Armenian Church. In spite of all tragic persecutions and dire massacres our church has preserved its religious and national identity and not merged with The Church of Rome, or with The Greek Orthodox Church. These churches have never ceased to persecute her because of religious animosities and dogmatic and theological differences. But "She passed with the Armenian people through all the vicissitudes of their political life; she was exposed to internal and external troubles and shocks, her body was wounded and torn, but in spite of all these trials she has maintained her national identity.

Political and dogmatic violences, whether it came from Rome, from Byzantium, or from Ktesiphon (from The Nestorian Church which was powerful under the Sassanides) could not shake her. She remained firm as Mount Ararat, in spite of the thunders which assailed her from all sides."*

Armenians from the beginning have remained attached in their doctrines to The Church of Alexandria. In The Ecumenical Council of Ephesus, held in 431, the doctrine of St. Cyril of Alexandria triumphed. He recognized ONE NATURE UNITED OF THE INCARNATE WORD. In the Incarnation of Jesus Christ, the two natures, the humanity and the divinity did not preserve their duality, because that would destroy the reality of His passion. The Incarnated Jesus has one Nature United—in Armenian: Miavorial mi bnouthiun—. In the person of Jesus Christ the divinity and the humanity were united without change or con-

* Page 10.

III

fusion forming One Nature or Unity. To quote Catholicos Papken: "Jesus Christ was perfect God and perfect man. The divinity and the humanity were united without confusion, forming one single nature in Jesus Christ."*

Catholicos Hovhan Otznetzi (+728), at The Armenian Council of Manzikert, 726 A. D. defined the problem as follows: "We confess One Nature of the Word Incarnate perfect God and perfect Man, united indivisibly, and inconfused unity."**

St. Nerses Shnorhaly, The Armenian Catholicos of the twelfth century writes: "One Nature in Christ means the indivisible and the ineffable union of the Word and the Flesh."

"After the union of two natures, the duality of natures could not exist in Him. . . . Therefore, we speak of One Nature as the inseparable and indivisible Union of human and divine natures, and not as confusion, and of two natures as inconfused, unchanged and not divided; both are within the limits of orthodoxy."***

The following paragraph is a quotation from the creed of the Armenian Church: "Who, for us men, and for our salvation, having come down from Heaven, was incarnate, became man, was born perfectly of the Holy Virgin Mary by the Holy Ghost. Of whom he took body, soul and

---

* Page 24.
** Page 224. (Book of Letters) (Գիրք Թղթոց)
*** Unthanragan Tooghtk Sourp Nersesy Shnorhalvo. (Letters general of St. Nerses Shnorhaly, printed in 1871, Jerusalem, Pages 96-97.)

mind and everything that is in man, verily and not in semblance."

Eutyches taught a blend and confusion of two natures, involving almost a disappearance of the human nature. He confessed two natures before the union, and one nature after the Incarnation.

On the other hand the Chalcedonian formula holds that the Incarnate Lord has two natures, human and divine. His humanity and divinity are separated; each nature preserves its peculiar property and acts accordingly. One is adorable, the other not, one of these shines forth in the miracles, and the other succumbs to injuries.

The Church of Armenia anathematizes the former and repudiates the latter. Her argument is evident. The Monophysitism of Eutyches being a confusion of two natures is infused unity in the Person of Christ. Eutyches went so far that even thought of a heavenly origin for the body of Christ. Therefore, with regard to his definition, because of the distinct separation of the two natures the Life, Passion, Crucifixion and Resurrection of Christ would lose their divine significance and would not have any saving value. Moreover, the formula of Chalcedon and the tome of Leo support the thesis of Nestorius which the Armenian Church rejects equally with the teaching of Eutyches.

The confession of the Armenian Church is very clear; it is that of an inconfused and harmonious unity of two distinct natures.

The Eutychian heresy is sometimes associated through ignorance rather than misapprehension, with the Church of Armenia. This is done particularly by those who have gained their knoweldge from Roman Catholic sources. Gibbon, an eminent English writer, says that, "The Armenians alone are the pure disciples of Eutyches, an unfortunate parent who has been renounced by the greater part of his spiritual progeny. They alone persevere in the opinion that the manhood of Christ was created, or existed without creation, of a divine and incorruptible substance."*

Gibbon and all those who copy him do not realize that the Church of Armenia for fifteen centuries pronounced anathemas against Eutyches and his followers. She also anathematized all those groups of heretics who are recognized as heresiarchs by the One Holy Universal Church. Moreover, The Armenian Church adopted the Athanasian creed which is in itself a refutation of Eutychianism.

Accordingly, we demand that the charge of Eutychian monophysitism, which is made "whether by ignorance or in fit of polemics" against the Church of Armenia, be corrected in the books of history. Moreover, the Chalcedonians must not represent her as schismatic, simply because she refused to accept the Chalcedonian definition. The Church of Armenia is a part of the One Holy Catholic Church. In essential points of doctrine she is in accord with the Roman and Greek Orthodox Churches.

---

* The Decline and Fall of Roman Empire by E. Gibbon, vol. v. page 158, London: Methuen and Co.; 1911.

Each church is at liberty to differ on points of secondary importance, provided that she maintain the fundamental principles of Christianity.

The Armenians did not enter into dogmatic and metaphysical quarrels nor into the secondary and endless doctrinal discussions which began after the division of the CHURCH, after The Third Ecumenical Council, and which have continued for centuries, weakening the CHURCH by causing constant uprising hatred between Christian Nations. Martyrdoms throughout her long history are a testimony to her part in keeping unquenched the light of Christianity.

Catholicos Papken, with regard to doctrinal controversies says: "It is necessary to admit frankly that theological disputes, controversies, and quarrels which the Christian nations have carried on between each other with more or less bitterness, have greatly impeded the expansion of the divine kingdom, and therefore they have prevented the full radiation of the divine light, the divine truth, and the divine love in human society."*

The Church of Armenia is a strongly nationalistic church in character, and the oldest of all national churches.** Since the official recognition

---

* Page 8.
** The conversion of the emperor Constantine took place in 313 A.D. By the edict of Milan he put Christianity and paganism in the Empire on the same level. But 12 years before his conversion, in 301 A.D. Christianity was established as the dominant and official state religion of Armenia. King Tiridates, the royal family, the princess, the high officers, the army and the people were converted to Christianity.

T. V. P.

of Christianity as a state religion in Armenia, at the beginning of the fourth century, until the present day the Armenian nation and The Armenian Church have been one and the same. The Church has been and is the center of Armenian national life. After the fall of the Armenian kingdom in Cilicia, in 1375, the nation centered all its cultural, literary, religious and political life within the Church. The political history of the nation coalesced with its church history. You cannot draw a line of distinction between the two. We Armenians are passionately attached to the venerable church of our ancestors. We owe to our church our identity as a nation after the terrible horrors and tortures of centuries. At the middle of the fifth century the Persians furiously attacked and devoured Armenia in order to annihilate Christianity. All their efforts was in vain. The chief Magian, who had come to Armenia to propagate Zoroastrism, wrote to his king in Persia as follows:—"The Christian religion among Armenians has been fused with their very bone and flesh, it is impossible to divide it." (Yeghishe). We believe that the persecution of our church is the consolidation of national union for the future as it has been in the past.

A study of the national constitution of the Armenians shows that there is no antagonism between laity and clergy. They do not form distinct separate classes as in The Church of Rome. The administration of the church is mostly in the hands of the laity. Priests, bishops, and patriarchs

VIII

are chosen by the people and are controlled by the congregation.

In other churches religion may be concerned with individual life only, but in the Armenian Church religion is blended with the social and national life. In the mind of many an Armenian it is The Church that makes The Armenian an Armenian. Archbishop Ormanian, in his book "The Church of Armenia" says:

"The national Church (of Armenia) has been the sole bond which has united the scattered remnants of the race of Haik in an indestructible bundle within her folds. She has unquestionably given them, not only the elements of inner vitality, but also the means whereby they could give themselves form and shape for the battle of life, and maintain themselves in their dealings and their efforts. She has fashioned them into a distinct body, the members of which ever possess that individuality which distinguishes them through space and time.

Bereft, for many centuries, of political life, the nation has linked herself to her church as to an anchor of salvation, and hence it is that she has been able to triumph over the difficulties which have assailed her, though she has emerged from those struggles in an enfeebled condition and in past exercised so potent an influence over her diminished numbers. That force which has in the past exercised so potent an influence over her destinies has not ceased to operate. She will resort to it as long as circumstances make it her duty to do so. Experience has shown that, in the absence of a political link, the national church is alone capable of making up for that universal want. She is the visible expression of the absent fatherland, the one that satisfies the noblest longings of the soul. . . . "

"Every good Armenian . . . has sought refuge in the bosom of his national church, which he wishes should remain intact, with her institutions, her prerogatives, and the integrity of her acquired privileges."

"He is impressed with the conviction that the church, which has protected him in the past, will continue to protect him in the future." (pp. 224-226).

The spirit of tolerance and liberalism has been characteristic of the Armenian Church. The Roman Church proclaims "WHOSOEVER IS BEYOND THE PALE OF THE ROMAN CHURCH HAS NO PART IN ETERNAL SALVATION". The Greek Orthodox Church begins to rebaptize and ordain as soon as she finds no strict conformity with her practices. But the Armenian Church on the contrary claims that each church is free to differ in secondarily important points and upholds that true universality is in the principle of In Necessariis Unitas, which embodies the fundamental principles of Christianity. From the early era she never held that those outside of her pale are deprived of eternal salvation. She has never as the Roman and Greek Churches have, threatened her flock with any chastisement in future life, if they broke away from her. This is due to

x

her spirit of tolerance and liberalism. She has been subject to aggression from various churches and to foreign proselytism. The sole intention of the aggression has been the undermining of the fabric of the Armenian Church. Catholic and Protestant missionaries have come to establish separate communities among the Armenians. To quote Patriarch Ormanian: "The Armenian Church has always understood the meaning of union in the true and strict sense of the term. She has desired to see its establishment on the basis of a spiritual communion between the churches of mutual respect for their several positions, of liberty for each within the limits of her own sphere, and the spirit of Christian charity overruling all. She has never tolerated that union should take the guise of dominion, nor be mistaken for proselytism." (The Church of Armenia, p. 58).

There has been always a bond of sympathy between the Armenian Church and The Anglican Communion, of which The Episcopal Church in America is a daughter. The late Armenian Catholicos of Etchmiadzin, Ephraim (+1830), the late Armenian Patriarch of Constantinople, Archbishop Nerses Varjabedian (+1884), the late Armenian Catholicos of Sis, Meguerditch Kefsizian (+1894), and the late Armenian Patriarch of Jerusalem, Haroutun Vehapetian (+1910), were always in friendly terms with the primates of the Church of England. Everybody knows of the fraternal relation of the late Armenian primate of the United States of America, Archbishop Tourian (+1933) with Bishop W. Manning of The Episcopal Church. In 1897, the late Catholicos Khrimian allowed Mr. Selian to be ordained to the priesthood for The Armenian Church in the United States of America by an American Episcopalian bishop. This position of Catholicos Khrimian towards The Episcopal Church shows the friendly relations between the two churches and the liberal spirit of the Armenian Church. Would the religious head of any other church allow an ordination by a bishop outside his own church?

This is an example of the broad understanding of Christianity in the Armenian Church. She has suffered and has been persecuted for her spirit of tolerance, and liberalism, but she is resolved to remain faithful and uphold these larger views unimpaired.

We have translated this concise volume in order to satisfy the desire of many an Armenian, especially of the new generation, who is passionately interested in the history of The Armenian Church. The translator will be rewarded if this little book can arouse a deep interest in the young generation of Armenians. We earnestly hope that it will stimulate also in the members of the Episcopal Church love and sympathy towards the oldest national church in the world.

Terenig Vartabed Poladian

The General Theological Seminary
175 Ninth Avenue
New York City
February 17th, 1939.

PREFACE TO THE SECOND EDITION

The copies of the first edition of "The Armenian Church", which appeared in May 1939, were exhausted two months after publication. Because of a great demand we gladly present the volume in its second edition.

This concise book aroused a great interest not only among the young Armenian English-speaking generation but also among the members of other Christian churches.

We believe that this second edition will further increase the interest and sympathy among English speaking peoples towards the church of Armenia which has diffused the Divine Light for two thousand years among the non-Christian peoples that have surrounded her.

Terenig Vartabed Poladian

July 25th, 1939
Chicago, Ill.

DEDICATED

to all those who desire to have

a clear and complete idea of

THE ARMENIAN CHURCH

her history, her dogmas and her rites.

PREFACE

Christianity is a revelation of true light in its origin, in its aim, and in its effects.

All the great religions, in which an ennobling ethic and a healthy attitude prevail have for their aim the happiness of Mankind.

The history of Religions shows that Christianity has contributed the most to the realization of the happiness of mankind, and still continues to do so.

Christianity is not the Church.

Christianity does not denote a great nation or a group of famous personages.

Christianity is not theology.

Christianity is not the ecclesiastical organization.

Christianity, according to its origin and aim, is a mode of teaching and of education, a rule of life to follow, a manner of living according to the Divine rule; in sum, it is the complete life of Man himself, or the perfect life, as the Lord said: "I came that they may have life, and may have it abundantly" (John 10:10), "Ye therefore shall be perfect, as your heavenly Father is perfect." (Matthew 5: 48).

History shows to us that it is precisely Christianity which has given to Mankind the surest means to develop the civilization of today and consolidate it as a unity.

What, therefore, is the Christian Church? Who are this people who by their activity have contributed to present day civilization and to the happiness of mankind?

If the dvinity is light, what is that christian church which succeeds in leading her people towards that light?

If the divinity is truth, what is that church which continues to educate with success her people in the spirit of truth?

If the divinity is peace, what is the church which has established and maintained peace, agreements, and solidarity between nations and peoples?

If God is love and if Jesus Christ is the concrete expression of that love in this world in his life and his Gospel, what is the church which became the guardian of love, of solidarity, of fraternity, of devotion, of sacrifice, on which depends the personal happiness of christians as well as that of the entire christian community?

It is necessary to admit frankly that theological disputes, controversies, and quarrels which the christian nations before have carried on between each other with more or less bitterness, have greatly impeded the expansion of the divine kingdom, and therefore they have prevented the full radiation of the divine light, the divine truth and the divine love in human society.

Those who have learned and been filled with the evangelical spirit, as it relates to men and

8

social groups, do not take into account, at least among important questions, the theology which Christians have professed, or the opulence of the church to which they belonged, or the luxury and authority which the chiefs of the churches enjoyed. In fact, according to Jesus Christ, it is not those who call him "Lord Lord" who are the real christians, but those who live like him, so as to establish the kingdom of heaven in the world (Matthew 7: 21-22 and Luke 6: 46, 13: 25).

Armenia is a small "plat-band", according to the picturesque expression of the Armenian historian, Moses of Khoren, which has often been subjugated to great powers; but this small "plat-band" has accomplished deeds of great value— warlike exploits and works consecrated to the prosperity of the country, to religious progress, and to cultural achievements such as literature, painting, sculpture, architecture and lastly a christian devotion admirable in spirit and practice.

One may observe, without forcing the truth, that the Armenian people is eminently a christian people. Her customs, the philosophical views which are natural to her, her daily life and lastly her social ideals—all these are deeply impregnated with the christian spirit. The Armenian Church has been the intrepid torch-bearer of the religion of Christ. She has lived this religion and has preached it, at the cost of her life, to the nations and peoples who surrounded her in the Near-East with a heterogeneous environment. This church is an apostolic heritage of the Armenian people.

Naturally she has proceeded with the Armenian people through all the vicissitudes of their political life; she was exposed to internal and external agitations and shocks, her body was wounded and torn, but in spite of these trials she has maintained her national identity.

Political and dogmatic violences whether it came from Rome, whether from Byzantium, or from Ktesiphon, (The Nestorian Church which was so powerful under the Sassanides,) could not shake her. She remained firm as Mount Ararat, in spite of the thunders which were assailing her from all sides.

Fortunately the theological zeal of those who, depending on political force, formerly did not cease to intimidate the Armenian Church, has forsaken them forever. Serious thinkers as well as intelligent believers, look at the actions of past centuries with an understanding smile. They are more tolerant, more inclined to respect the religious conscience of other people—which is more humane and more conformable to the christian spirit.

We have stressed this fact, and we believe we should insist upon it again.

The christian churches should draw together and fill themselves with the spirit of cooperation and love, because the present danger threatens Christianity itself. It is not the churches of this or that denomination which are persecuted but religion itself is in peril. Formerly, states and governments protected the Church and used her for political and diplomatic purposes. Nowadays, governments, with some exceptions, ignore religion or persecute it openly.

All the Christian Churches, small or great, should form a single front against the common dangers which arise from indifference, from the neglect of religious teaching, from atheism, from the intolerance of one church towards another, etc. No separate church will be able to do anything without this one front. If the churches of diverse denominations continue to rise up one against another in open or secret struggle, if they continue using all means in order to encroach on other flocks, certainly none of these churches will be able to maintain its authority sheltered from these assaults.

This kind of behavior is contrary to what our Lord said: "For he that is not against you is for you." (Luke 9: 50). It may be considered as a kind of conspiracy of the religions themselves against the Church. It serves only to ruin Christianity and helps the efforts that are made from without against religion.

Since The Great War, The Armenian Church has been passing through a critical stage. Soviet Armenia and republican Turkey have condemned her to sterility. In the diaspora, she is in danger of decay.

One of the most important parts of the Armenian Church, victim of the Great War, is established in Lebanon and in Syria.

We are sure that these pages will strengthen the bonds which have been formed between the Armenian Church and other churches during the six years since the establishment of the seat of the Catholicossate of Cilicia in Lebanon. . . . .

We hope that these pages will serve to assure to this already existing bond a lasting stability by stimulating a new current of sympathy, created by an exact knowledge, towards the Church of Armenia.

PAPKEN I.
Coadjuter Catholicos of Cilicia.

THE CHURCH OF ARMENIA

The Church of Armenia is one of the branches of the Christian Church. It was founded and organized in Armenia.

Armenia is a mountainous country between 37° - 49° longitude and 37½° - 41¾° latitude north.

These are her historical boundaries, which were enlarged or narrowed according to the courage and power of her rulers.

The historic Armenia, HAYK, was divided into two principal parts: Greater Armenia in the east and Lesser Armenia in the west. The Taurus, Mesopotamia, the Caucasus, the Caspian Sea and Georgia formed her boundaries.

Mountains and plateaus are the characteristic features of Armenia. The highest mountain is Ararat, mentioned in the Bible. (II Kings 19: 37, Isaiah 37: 38 and Jeremiah 51: 27).*

---

* The name of the mountain of Ararat is also associated with "The Land of Armenia" (In Armenian: Araratian Ashkhar). The first two passages speak of the escape of Adrammelech and Sharezen "into the Land of Ararat" after assassinating their own father, Sennacherib.

In the third passage the prophet Jeremiah summons the forces of Armenia to combine with the Medes to overthrow Babylon, in following words: "Set ye up a standard in the land, blow the trumpet among the nations, prepare the nations against her, call together against her the kingdoms of Ararat, Minni and Ashkenaz; appoint a marshal against her."

The greatest river of Armenia is the Arax (Yeraskh), which before flowing into the Caspian Sea unites with the river Kour (Cyprus), which separates Armenia from Georgia; the Euphrates and Tigris have their sources in Armenia, cross Mesopotamia, and flow into the Persian Gulf.

Greater Armenia has always been exposed to the influence of Iranian civilization, and Lesser Armenia to that of Byzantine civilization; so that because of her geographical situation which put her between two great empires of the east and of the west, Armenia was prevented from developing an altogether independent civilization. She has had several national dynasties, and at a favorable moment, she rose to the height of her glory, and under the reign of Tigranes The Great, was able to dictate the fate of Western Asia.

Christianity penetrated into Armenia when she enjoyed a relative independence under the reign of her national kings of the Arsacide family.

Phrenological and particularly linguistic studies have proved that the Armenians belong to the Indo-European race. The Armenian language occupies a separate place among the Indo-Euroean languages. According to the generally accep-

From the Assyrian inscriptions we learn that the earliest name of Armenia, by which it was known to the Hebrew and Assyrian writers, was Ararat. In the story of the deluge Gen. 8:4 "The Ark of Noah, rested upon the mountains of Ararat." This quotation shows clearly that the author of the Book of Genesis is accurate in his knowledge of the fact that Ararat is the name of the country upon whose mountains the ark of Noah rested.   T. V. P.

ted opinion, the Armenians are a Phrygian colony which came to settle in Armenia.

The Armenians call their people HAY and their country HAYK, whence a national legend, preserved by Moses of Khoren has formed the eponym Hayk.

The pre-christian religion of Armenia was paganism. Armenia had seven principal pagan sanctuaries, of which the most famous ones were in Yeriz (at present Yerzinga or Yerzindjan) in the district of Akiliseh on the banks of the Euphrates and in Daron, in the region of Moush.

The divinities Aramazd, Anahit, Astghik, Vahagn were famous for their magnificent temples, and their worship was popular all over the country.

●

DAWN OF CHRISTIANITY IN ARMENIA

The Armenians have beautiful traditions to explain the propagation of Christianity among them.

1. Among the pagans who wanted to meet Christ through Philip, there were some who were Armenians (John 12: 20-23). These verses of John are in harmony with the legend of Abgar. The Armenians considered the kings of Osroen (Edessa), who possessed a part of Southern Armenia, as having been also their kings, and claim by

this fact to have known Christ, even before the dispersion of the apostles.

2. Tertulien, the famous father of the Latin Church, in his commentaries on the well known passage of the Acts of the Apostles (2:8-11) believes that it is possible to insert the names of the Armenians among the names of the first proselytes.*

This conjecture seems to us very probable, because in Armenia, as in all countries of the Near East, there had always been Jewish colonies who were scattered among the nations of the country.

In any case, pre-evangelical and pre-apostolic legends prove that Armenia, thanks to her geographical and political position, was well acquainted with the great events which were taking place in neighbouring countries.

If Asia Minor and Mesopotamia had sent to Jerusalem Jewish pilgrims for the Passover, would not interested Jews or Armenians have been able to go to the city of David in order to attend the universally known feast?

3. The apostolic preaching.

Almost all of the Christian Churches by tradition claim to be founded by one or several apostles. The Armenian Church has also her traditions,

---

*For whom have the nations believed, Parthians, Medes, Elamites, and they who inhabit Mesopotamia ARMENIA, Phrygia, Cappadocia and they who dwell in Pontus, etc. "An Answer to the Jews" vol. III. Book VII, page 217-218. Edinburgh T. and T. Clark, 38, George St. MDCCCLXX.

In his footnote on Acts 2:8-11, p. 300 Eberhard Nestle (Novum Testamentum Gracea) indicates that St. Augustine also read ARMENIA for Judea. T. V. P.

which make her origins go back to the Apostles Thaddeus and Bartholomew.

The apostle Thaddeus has been identified with one of the characters of the legend of Abgar, particularly Addai. Contemporary criticism has debated the veracity of this legend.

No doubt philology has its rights. But, in fact, its criticism deals less with the worth of the tradition than with the literary form with which it is clothed. A document such as the legend of Abgar may be without chronological and historical detail or composed in imitation of legends of the same sort, borrowing forms and literary methods. All of this need not make us surrender the genuine nucleus of the legend. So, H. Gelzer, an incontestable authority on the subject, is right in maintaining that traditions concerning Thaddeus are quite evidently much more ancient than the legend.

The preaching of Thaddeus is attested by the historian Faustus of Byzance, who wrote the History of Armenia of the fourth century.

In Armenia, the legend of Bartholomew is as old and popular as the legend of Thaddeus. According to a tradition, the monastery of Ardaz is founded upon the tomb of Thaddeus; it is called "The Seat of Thaddeus"; whereas the foundation of the monastery of "Hokiatz" is attached to the name of Bartholomew.

We shall not speak of the other apostles who had been in Armenia and are mentioned by the Armenian writers of the Middle Ages.

4. Latin testimonies tell us of the existence of Martyrs called "Martyrs of Ararat" (Alishan, "Arshalouys" pp. 70-71).

5. Eusebius* speaks about Mehruzanes, bishop of Armenians about 260, to whom St. Dionysius of Alexandria addressed a letter on penitence.

All these legendary and historical data prove that the Gospel of Christ was preached in Armenia from the time of the apostles, as our Lord instructed them: "Go ye therefore, and make disciples of all the nations, baptizing them into the name of the Father and of the Son and of the Holy Spirit: Teaching them to observe all things whatsover I commanded you." (Matthew 28: 19-20.

●

---

* "And he wrote to those in ARMENIA, likewise ON RE-PENTANCE, whose bishop was Mehruzanes." Eusebius Ecclesiastical History, vol. II Page 129, London: William Heinemann Ltd. New York: G. P. Putnam's Sons MCMXXXII. Eusebius gives further information about the Armenians, which shows that in the beginning of our era the light of Christianity had shone in Armenia: "In addition to this, the tyrant (Maximin Daia) had the further trouble of the war against the Armenians, men who from ancient times had been friends and allies of the Romans; but as they were Christians and exceedingly earnest in their piety towards the Deity, this hater of God by attempting to compel them to sacrifice to idols and demons, made of them foes instead of friends and enemies instead of allies." Vol. II, p. 351.

OFFICIAL RECOGNITION OF CHRISTIANITY
IN ARMENIA

History tells us that Christianity was severely persecuted in Palestine, its cradle, as well as in the rest of the Roman Empire.

The first victims were Jesus Christ himself, St. Stephen, and many others, as the Acts of Apostles attests.

Armenia also knew persecutions and had her martyrs. Princess Sandoukht, daughter of King Sanatrouk, first attained the crown of martyrs, with the apostles Thaddeus who had converted her.

From this time on until the third century, in Armenia as in other places, Christianity continued its clandestine existence, always in danger of persecution.

When Constantine the Great officially recognized the new faith and proclaimed liberty of conscience, the light of the Gospel shone everywhere. Religion coming out of obscure corners, and the catacombs shone with all its brightness, and the brilliant sun of the Christian faith followed the dawn.

At this time, Tiridates II, of the Arsacide line, was reigning in Armenia. He had received a pagan and Roman education, but later he abandoned the faith of his ancestors and embraced that of Jesus Christ.

He has the honour to have been the first Christian king. St. Gregory the Illuminator, who was also of the Arsacide race, after converting King Tiridates, used the favor of his royal disciple in order to continue his apostolic mission. The organzation of The Armenian Church is the work of St. Gregory the Illuminator.

By its conversion, Armenia entered into a new phase of civilization. The Armenian Church has the great merit of having preserved the national integrity, when after the loss of its political independence, Armenia was divided between the great empires which surrounded her.

It is the Armenian Church which gave the Armenian people the alphabet and the efficient instruments of civilization, which enabled the nation to cultivate the language and create an original literature.

St. Sahak, the great Catholicos, St. Mesrob, the eminent doctor, and Vramshabouh, the king of Armenia, are a distinguished triade whose harmony and foresight gave the Armenians that imperishable instrument, culture, for which literature stands.

In what manner and under what forms was Christian worship practiced in Armenia from the time of the Apostles Thaddeus and Bartholomew until St. Gregory the Illuminator? We do not know. Perhaps prayers as well as psalms were taught by heart. But from the time of St. Gregory the Illuminator until the invention of the Armenian alphabet, according to historians the Greek and Syriac languages were used.

After the invention of the alphabet the chief works of the Syrian and Greek Fathers were translated into Armenian. The Bible is the masterpiece of these translations.* In a short time a rich literature flourished.

The language of this literature is classical Armenian, called "grabar", meaning "written language", in order to distinguish it from vernacular Armenian or "Ashkharabar", the language of the people. Ancient Armenian was the literary language until the nineteenth century. At present it is used only in Church services and in the correspondence of the Armenian Patriarchate. In the nineteenth century from the common language, which has several dialects and a multitude of accents, a new literary language was drawn up, based on the old one. Today, it has been perfected as an instrument of modern thought. Unfortunately the political conditions in Armenia, divided as it is between two empires, have produced a sad bifurcation in modern literary Armenian and have forced it to follow two lines of development, one in Constantinople and the other in the Caucasus. In this way, we possess two literary languages.

The language of our school books, newspapers, reviews and of everyday affairs is modern Armenian.

The Armenian alphabet is composed of thirty-six letters. All the written characters are pronounced.

---

* Eminent scholars consider the Armenian translation of the Bible "The Queen of Translations."   T. V. P.

THE DOCTRINE OF THE ARMENIAN CHURCH

The Armenian Church confesses the doctrine which was approved and formulated by the first three ecumenical councils, and which is summed up in the Creed of Nicea and Constantinople.

This creed of faith is publicly and solemnly recited every morning in The Armenian Church. Remaining united with the ecumenical church in the essential points of the same dogma, she is thus a member of the Apostolic, Universal and One Church of Jesus Christ, as are all other churches great or small, which hold the same creed.

In dogmatics, the Armenian Church has remained faithful to the ideas of the period of 325. to 432 when Christian peoples and nations had not given a national character to their churches, when equality of power and authority prevailed between patriarchal sees, when emperors and kings had not yet forced their claims too far and exercised over the episcopal sees which depended on them their power and their personal prestige.

When the political authorities meddled unduly with religious questions, the principle of equality and Chrstian love came close to disappearing and all sorts of ambitions which supplanted it, nearly banished peace and honest thought from the Christian Church.

Bishops, relying on the states which protected them, began to claim ascendancy one upon another and vied for supremacy.

With this kind of aspiration is connected the tendency of this or that to reserve to itself competency in what concerns the doctrines and customs of the church. Above all it was the see of Rome which aspired in this matter to exclusive competency and authority. Thereby, The Church of Christ, One and Universal, while maintaining the unity of the faith and its universality, fell administratively into pieces. Every people, every nation, communicated to its own church a nationalistic impress, whence resulted the local variations in the bosom of the same One and Universal Christian Church.

A differentiation of this sort seemed indeed altogether natural, and it would properly become more marked in the course of time under the influence of diverse conditions which create the geography, the language, the civilization and lastly the customs of each country.

Unfortunately it was not this proper and useful differentiation that developed; the rivalry between the episcopal sees was transformed into hatred, after they attempted to pronounce on dogmatical questions and to impose with an unjustified pretention their interpretations upon those who did not share them. They even had the audacity to resort to the secular forarm, to take advantage of political powers for persecuting their adversaries, to the detriment of the unity and universality of the Church of Christ.

It is heart-rending for the Christians to see how the simplicity of the apostolic age, the harmonious life which prevailed in the time of the first three ecumenical councils, degenerated and gave way to hatred, to the passion for domination and for command. In consequence, christian rose up against christian armed with all that was unforgivable and anti-christian as well in its essence as in its particular manifestations.

The Armenian Church was dragged into the struggle on the occasion of the Chalcedonian controversies which rent the Church in the fifth and sixth centuries. Whatever were the reasons for the abstention of the Armenians from the Council of Chalcedon, held in 451, they did not adopt the decisions of this council. At Chalcedon it was not a question of combatting a heresy like those of Arius, Macedonius and Nestorius. The first three ecumenical councils had discussed the controversies concerning God the Father, The Son, and The Holy Ghost, and had given a dicisive solution in very precise formulas. The problem which was propounded in the council of Chalcedon had interest only for subtle theologians, who reconsidering the teaching of Nestorius, wanted to introduce more precision in the mystery of incarnation, namely in the mode of the union of two natures of Jesus Christ. Cyril of Alexandria, the adversary of Nestorius, had already decided the question by his famous formula: ONE NATURE UNITED OF THE INCARNATE WORD. Jesus Christ was perfect God and perfect man. The divinity and the humanity were united without confusion, forming one single nature in Jesus **Christ.**

24

The members of the council of Chalcedon were not satisfied with the Cyrilian formula which had been adopted and confirmed at the council of Ephesus. They opened the question of the two natures. May we not say that the opposition to Cyril disguised in fact the blow which they wanted to give to the prestige of the see of Alexandria? It was natural that Pope Leo (440-461), took advantage of the occasion to publish his Tome, his famous dogmatic letter, in which he rather dictated a decision by authority than discussed the question. The conception which the pope expounded of the union of the two natures, of which each one, according to him, maintained its proper faculties, and had its proper operation, appeared rather to support the thesis of Nestorius rather than that of Cyril.

Pope Leo triumphed at Chalcedon, but peace was not thereby established in the Church. The Chalcedonians decreed the formula of two natures against that of one nature, at a time when the latter was somewhat compromised by the teaching of Eutyches, who had tightened the union of natures up to the point of the absorption, after the incarnation, of one by the other, the human nature by the divine, resulting in a dissolution or confusion of the two natures, whereas with Cyril the union was conceived of as without confusion and without mingling.

So the Council if Chalcedon embattled Eutychianism, and not the christological doctrine of Cyril. For the patriarch of Alexandria nature indicates a separate and independent existence; therefore the conception of two natures involves the affirmation of two persons. So the Armenian Church, which holds firmly to the christology of Cyril, has not ceased to regard the two natures of Chalcedon as a kind of Nestorianism. The Chalcedonians, for their part, have often imputed Eutychianism to the Armenians, whether by ignorance or in a fit of polemics. In fact Eutyches has always been anathematized by the Armenians.

Some would like to consider the Armenian Church monophysite. She may be so regarded, but with the patriarch Cyril, and in the sense that the Christological teaching of this famous theologian is monophysite, because Armenian christology is based on the school of Alexandria.

In sketching briefly the dogmatic basis of the Armenian Church, we by no means intend to renew controversies which have no interest for the public and which have long since belonged to the domain of history. But this which is most significant in the past history of the Armenian Church, is an important fact which must be taken into consideration even in our days.

From the moment when the Armenian Church obtained her administrative independence, she elaborated her theology, her rites, her traditions. She has known how to defend herself against all attacks with a firmness and perseverance worthy of admiration. Byzantium caused her many injuries. Its emperors often attacked her and persecuted her with an incomprehensible fanaticism. Later, from the time of the Crusades, it was Rome which took up the Byzantine policy and which has continued her efforts until our own days to restore "the lost sheep" of the Armenian Church into the fold of catholicism. One need not hesitate to say that the question is less one of saving the souls rather than of submitting them to the authority of Rome. Is there any reason to destroy a church, which is one of the oldest churches, and one which has truly merited the cross of Jesus Christ through the blood of her martyrs, by a roll of martyrs unequalled in the annals of humanity? The doctrinal differences certainly are no reason for arming one church against another. Christian theology and the principles of the Christian faith are different things. The first, whatever form it takes, should not be an obstacle to a harmonious collaboration, based on the Christian faith. The Armenian Church in defending herself has never attacked the conscience of others. She has always preached tolerance for that which separates churches, love and agreement in that which unites them. Such was and is her motto. Why therefore ruin this small but glorious fortress of the Christian ideal?

●

THE DIVINE OFFICE
IN THE ARMENIAN CHURCH

In the Armenian Church the divine office is rich, not only in its contents, but in its form (rites and ceremonies).

The daily service is found prescribed in the "Geamakirk" (book of hours), which contains a cycle of nine hours, divided into three groups:

a. Night, dawn and morning service.

b. Third, Sixth and Ninth Hour service.

c. Evening, Compline, and Requiem Service.

The services of the hours are devoted to the Holy Trinity or to one of the three persons, to the memory of Jesus Christ and to the mysteries of the faith.

The daily service of the Armenian Church is composed of psalms, canticles in imitation of psalms, chants and readings from the Holy Scriptures.

The division of nine hours is apparently a monastic system; the service of every hour is to be celebrated at its own proper hour. Later, they have been rearranged into three groups.

The service of each hour begins and ends with the Lord's Prayer.

MASS

At present, in the Armenian Church, the Holy Communion is not celebrated every day either solemnly or by the priest alone.

Nowadays the custom is to celebrate Holy Communion in cities on Sundays, Holidays and as needed in particular circumstances such as marriages, funerals and requiems.

The Holy Communion cannot be celebrated twice in the same day. It is not allowed to celebrate it simultaneously on different altars in the same church. The priest can celebrate only one Mass per day.

For the Holy Communion, pure wine (without water) is used, and unleavened bread as in The Roman Church. The faithful receive the eucharist in both kinds. The priest dips the Host in the chalice of wine and breaking it into pieces, puts a piece of it in the mouth of the communicant.

The holy eucharist is kept in the church. The priests can carry it to communicate the sick, in cases of emergency.

THE BAPTISM

Old tradition desired that infants should be baptized eight days after their birth; but there are exceptions to this rule in practice.

Immediately after baptism, confirmation is administered followed by Holy Communion, which consists of touching the lips with the eucharist.

The candidate must have a god-father.

The baptized is dressed in white.

Baptism, according to the old Armenian tradition, is conferred in Church, in fonts which are situated on the north side. But in case of need, baptism can also be conferred in houses, especially during time of emigration.

Extreme unction is given with the same Holy Oil as Confirmation.

Only the deceased clergymen receive extreme unction, on their foreheads and on their right hand.

CHURCH ORDER

Ordination in the Church is performed by the Bishop.

The Armenian Church possesses all the orders known in other churches. The functions of the lower orders are often performed by young men aspiring to the priesthood.

Secular and regular clergy are distinguished from each other; the one is married, the other celibate.

The regular priest, the monk, is ordinarily called "Vartabed" (doctor).

The priest, the bishop, and the catholicos receive unction after ordination.

The priest is ordained by the bishop, and the bishop by the catholicos, assisted by two bishops.

The catholicos is usually ordained by twelve bishops.

The patriarchs of Constantinople and of Jerusalem have neither ordination nor consecration.

They are bishops and after their election to the patriarchal seat, they become arch-bishops ipso facto.

For reasons of solemnity, all the ordinations, from deacon to catholicos take place during the Holy Communion.

In the ordination of a deacon and a priest it is the ordaining bishop himself who celebrates the mass, in the ordination of a bishop, it is the ordaining catholicos, and in the ordinaton of the catholicos, the catholicos himself celebrates the mass.

The secular clergy are parish priests, deacons and sub-deacons, and are in charge of parishes.

The "Vartabeds" and the bishops are supported by the Church.

SOME FURTHER POINTS

The officiant prepares himself to celebrate The Holy Communion by prayers, accompanied by fasting and vigil. Married priests must abstain from conjugal intercourse. In some regions, they had to stay fifteen days in the church.

The faithful must be fasting to receive Holy Communion. They are free to communicate whenever they wish, so long as they have confessed to the priest.

Generally the congregation communicates at five great feasts: Christmas, Easter, Transfiguration, Assumption, and Exaltation of The Cross. It is particularly at Christmas and Easter that the Armenian people communicate with great religious fervour.

A couple desiring to marry must receive Holy Communion.

Funeral ceremonies are held in houses, in churches and in cemeteries.

Armenians bury their dead. Nowadays, because of new conditions of life, especially in America and in Europe the rich people bury their dead in crypts or cremate them.

DAYS OF FEAST AND OF ABSTINENCE

The feasts are divided in two groups:

a. Dominical feasts.

b. Feasts of Martyrs.

The dominical feasts are those which relate to to the person of Jesus and to his memory, such as Christmas and Easter.

The feasts of the martyrs relate to saints.

The Armenian calendar distinguishes fixed and movable feasts. The fixed feasts are those whose date is determined and annexed to a day of a month. Their number is very limited.

a. The Nativity and Epiphany, 6th of January.

b. The Circumcision, 13th of January.

c. Candlemas, 14th of February.

d. The Annunciation, 7th of April.

These four feasts are ancient. The following three are relatively recent.

e. The Conception, 9th of December.

f. The Nativity of the Blessed Virgin, 8th of September.

g. The Purification, 21st of November.

All the other feasts are movable. They are arranged according to the weeks and divided among four days: Monday, Tuesday, Thursday and Saturday. They depend on the oscillation of Easter over thirty-five days.

The Assumption and The Exaltation of The Cross have fixed days: the 15th of August and the 14th of September. But in order to give them more solemnity they are transferred to the Sunday nearest these dates.

The feast of the Appearance of the Cross, formerly fixed at the 7th of March, has been transferred to the fifth week after Easter.

The Armenian Church has days and weeks of abstinence. The days are Wednesday and Friday. The weeks are those which precede the great feasts. In addition, she observes the great Lent.

It is not customary to commemorate the saints on the days of abstinence, except in certain weeks which do not precede the great feasts and on the Saturdays of Lent.

The days of abstinence are assigned for penitence and have special services.

Wednesdays are particularly assigned for penitence, and Fridays to requiem and to the commemoration of the death.

The Armenian Church has 120-130 days in the year reserved for the commemoration of Saints, and 150-157 days for abstinence and penitence.

The feast of every Saint is celebrated alone, but sometimes certain feasts are celebrated together because of their moving.

IMPORTANT NOTE

The list of saints adopted by the Armenian Church contains besides The Fathers of the first three universal councils more than 200 names which belong to the Christian Church of the Second to Sixth centuries, and a limited number of Armenian saints.

The fact that the Armenian Church has adopted so many saints who belong to the ancient church proves that she is an old member of the One Uuniversal Church of Christ. St. Gregory the Illuminator, the organizer of the Armenian Church, is venerated by all the churches.

The saints of the Old Testament, and those who are contemporary with Christ, as well as the celestial powers are commemorated in the Armenian Church, under the name of saints OLD AND NEW, KNOWN AND UNKNOWN. She also venerates all the martyrs of the Universal Church whose names are inscribed in the Book of Life.

Finally, with a broad Christian spirit and with a true religious devotion, which is native to the Armenian Church, she prays every day for the conservation and prosperity of the christian faith, and for the reign of peace over all the world.

THE ARMENIAN BIBLE

Two famous fathers of the Armenian Church, the Catholicos Sahak, grandson of St. Gregory the Illuminator, and St. Mesrop, under the auspices of King Vramshabouh, succeeded in inventing the Armenian alphabet at the very beginning of the fifth century, and began to translate the Holy Scriptures.

In 432, after the council of Ephesus, those pupils of St. Sahak and St.Mesrop, who had been sent to Byzantium to perfect themselves in the Greek language in order to translate the works of the Church Fathers, returned with an excellent copy of the Septuagint. They corrected the translation made from the Septuagint and went on to translate all the rest; thus all was translated, from Genesis to the Book of Revelation and put in circulation.

The Bible and especially the New Testament, became the favorite books of the Armenian people.

The oldest copies of theBible which have reached us do not go back beyond the twelfth century. The manuscripts of the gospels are more numerous and there are some that date from the Ninth century. In order to form an idea of the biblical education of the old Armenians, it suffices to recall the testimony of the historian Stephen Orpelian, Archbishop of Sunig (+1304), that in his diocese alone there were about 10,000 copies of the Holy Scriptures.

THE PRINTED BIBLE

The invention of Gutenberg interested the Armenians very early. In 1512 they already had printed some works in Venice.

The first edition of the Bible in the Armenian language was published in Amsterdam in 1666, by the order of the Catholicos James and under the direction of Archbishop Oskan of Erivan.

This is a fine illustrated edition; some copies were printed on parchment, one of which is in Jerusalem in the library of the Armenian Monastery of Saint James.

We cannot consider this a careful edition although it was reprinted in 1705, in Constantinople. Abbot Mekhitar, the founder of the Mekhitarist order of Venice, published in 1733 a better edition. But the best edition is that of Father John Zohrabian's published in 1805. Then the Bible was published in Saint Petersburg in 1817, in Serampore in 1817, and in Venice in 1860. This last edition was carried out by Fr. Arsen Bagradouni of the Mekhitarist order, who is well known for his thorough knowledge of the Armenian language.

The Pentateuch was published separately in 1892, in Constantinople, at the expense of The American Bible Society. The same society published the whole Bible according to the Hebrew Canon in 1895, in Constantinople. In 1902, at Etchmiadzin, Armenia, they began to publish a critical edition, but political events prevented the continuance of publication.

Old and New Testaments in Modern Armenian and Turkish, the latter in Armenian characters, have been several times published since 1890 by American and English Bible Societies, in New York, Constantinople, and Smyrna.

The Armenians are very fond of reading the Bible. From the very beginning, almost at the same time as the translation of the Bible, commentaries on Holy Scriptures, such as the works of St. Ephrem and St. John Chrysostom, were translated. The doctors of the Armenian church have also composed works of the same type, some of which are very recent.

THE BIBLE IN THE SERVICE

The reading of the Bible is well arranged in the Armenian Church. Pericopes, the lessons for reading, are assigned for each day in the year; they are divided into three groups: prophetic, apostolic and evangelic. On some days more than one lesson from the same group is read; sometimes the prophetic and apostolic lessons are omitted; but the gospel selections are always read.

All these lessons are brought together in a volume called "Djashotz". It is so called because the passages which it contains are read generally during the hours of meals,* except in some par-

---

* Among Armenians it is a widespread custom to have their meals after morning services.　　　　　T. V. P.

ticular and solemn cases when they are read in the morning and in the evening.

We should also note that the lessons of the Holy Scriptures, designed to be read at baptism, marriage and at funerals, etc. form in like manner a ritual book which is called "Mashtotz".

PREACHING IN THE ARMENIAN CHURCH

Preaching is held in high esteem by the Armenians; sermons are delivered in modern Armenian. The subject of the sermon is almost always taken from the Bible and it is constructed according to the model of the homelies of Saint John Chrysostom. A theme is selected from the Bible, explained and commented on.

The sermon generally follows the readings of the prophets and of the apostles. After the sermon the Gospel is read and then The Creed.

During the mass the sermon can be delivered directly before the Lord's Prayer.

Not long ago sermons were delivered chiefly during Lent, on Sundays and Thursdays. The latter one was for women.

The dominical feasts and those of Saints may furnish subjects for sermons.

The sermon at present is based upon a biblical theme, or upon a religious and moral subject adopted to the daily needs of the people.

The right of preaching is reserved to "Vartabeds", who have the necessary competency and erudition for understanding the doctrine of the Church and for making it understood.

RELIGIOUS LITERATURE

The Fathers of the Armenian Church, before and after the complete translation of the Bible, or simultaneously, translated the religious works of the famous Fathers of the Greek and Syrian Churches, as well as their historical and philosophical works. Thanks to these translations "The Synoptic" of St. Ephraim and "The Chronicle" of Eusebius have been preserved, the original texts being lost.

Beginning with the Fifth Century the following were translated into Armenian: Ephrem, Basil, Gregory Nazianzen, Athanasius, Chrysostom, Cyprian, the two Cyrils, Aphraates, (Persian Sage), Eusebius, Philop, etc., etc.

NATIONAL LITERATURE

The national literature of the Armenian people is no less rich. The historical and religious branches have been particularly cultivated.

Moses of Khoren is considered as the father of Armenian literature.

Armenian scholars, as well as European scholars interested in Armenian, have made the history of the Armenians known in Europe, either by translation of authors, by research, and laborious studies. French, English, German, Austrian, Russian and Armenian scholars have devoted themselves to Armenian research and have largely conrtibuted to making the Armenian civilization known to the learned world.

DENOMINATIONS IN THE
ARMENIAN CHURCH

Byzantium and Rome tried by all means to subdue The Armenian Church administratively and doctrinally.

The history of these struggles is sad reading.

The policy of Byzantium was not entirely sterile. Many Armenians accepted the doctrine of the Greek Church. They are called Horom (Greek) Armenians; this means that in origin and language they are Armenians, but in confession of faith Greek. After the catastrophe of 1915, the number of the Armenians of this type diminished little by little. At present we know nothing of their condition or of their number.

The Church of Rome was not less persistent in its efforts to Romanize the Armenians. The means which she used were not less severe.

Armenian kings of Cilicia, at critical moments of the country's history, professed a desire to comply with the demands of Rome. Sometimes even the Armenian clergy, willing or unwilling, supported the opportunism of the Court. But this tendency, before being fully realized, disappeared with the hope of thus preventing the destruction of the Cilician kingdom.

In the fourteenth century, under the auspices

of Pope John XXII, Bartholomew of Bologna was sent to Persia charged with an apostolic mission. He was an energetic and skillful preacher; he learned Persian and Armenian. He established a monastery and a school in Armenia. Young Armenian clergymen who sought after instruction gathered around him. Among these clergymen John of Kerny and James were fascinated by their master and multiplied the number of their adherents. From this time on dates the systematic penetration of Roman missionaries among the Armenians.

The movement known under the name of Uniates, which had for its purpose the Union of the Armenian Church with that of Rome, owes its origin to Bartholomew.

The fame of Rome, whcih played a great role in that time in European politics attracted many Armenians; among them were even high ecclesiastical dignitaries who entered into relations with the popes, and lavished promises to promote the cause of union, always in the hope of bettering the political situation in their country by the influence and protection of the popes.

The Armenians, being exposed to the dangers and menaces of the infidels, were ready to make every concession in order to assure their political existence.

This fact is proved by the report of Leonardo Abel, Archbishop of Sidon and legate of the pope, Gregory XII, who had sent him to Cilicia in 1583, in order to encourage the union between the Armenians and Rome.

Leonardo worked hard for the success of his mission. He held conversations with the Catholicoses Azaria and Khachadour of Cilicia as well as with Armenian courtiers. Finally, he realized that there was no chance of converting the Armenians before the pope had guaranteed the inviolability of their political and national life.

Leonardo wrote his report in Italian and sent it to Pope Sixtas V (+1590), successor to Gregory XII.

The French translation of this report appeared in la revue de l'Orinet Chretien, (1898 pp. 202-203 and 328-334). The answer of the Armenians is clear:

"Deliver us from the tyranny under which we live, then we shall become Latins (Catholic); you will be then the masters of our bodies and our souls and we shall do whatever you command".

The papacy was not in condition to give satisfaction to Armenians; so the Armenian people rejected the approaches of the pope. Certainly, some individuals of the laity as well as of the clergy adhered to Rome by reason of interest or in some cases perhaps through conviction.

It will not be superfluous to cite the observation made upon this subject by the eminent German scholar, H. Gelzer, who was at the same time a notable authority in the Armenian language and history and consequently a person entirely competent on the subject. "There have been some Armenians united with the Roman Church since the time of the Crusades and the Uniates, and also some from recent times, but they do not make much progress. Several patriarchs of Etchmiadzin and of Sis have had relations with Rome. The authenticity of their declaration of submission is not to be relied upon and its genuineness is certainly doubtful" (C. F. Armenian translation of P. Kalemkiarian, National Library XXV p. 71).

In any case, the Armenians of the Roman rite had to conceal their religious faith so as not to be exposed to the persecutions of the Turkish government as apostates or rebels to the spiritual authority. They were forced to leave Constantinople for the Asiatic provinces. Finally, the government of Sultan Mahmoud, because of the intervention of the European powers, recognized these converted Armenians as KATOLIK MILLET, (Catholic Nation) as a community independent of the Armenian Patriarchate, and they were placed under the authority of their own archbishop in 1830.

Another movement had begun a long time before the event that we have just related. The bishop of Aleppo, Abraham Arzivian had adhered to the Roman Church though he was the spiritual head of the Armenians in Aleppo.

In 1735-6, Arzivian and his adherents purchased the monastery of Mar George Avkar in Lebanon. They constituted a religious order according to the statute of the maronite monks of Saint Anthony; in 1749, they occupied Zmmar and there established their seat.

On the 26th day of November, 1740, Abraham Arzivian was proclaimed patriarch. In 1742, he went to Rome, where he received the pallium, on the 8th of December, from pope Benedict XIV, with the title of Patriarch of Cilicia. The following year, on his return from Rome, Arzivian wanted to pass through Constantinople, but he was prevented by the Armenian patriarch. He died in 1749. His successors were James Hovsepian, Mishel Kasbarian, Basil Askadian, Gregory Kupelian and Gregory Djeranian, under the names of Peter I, II, III, IV, V, VI.

The patriarchs of Lebanon did not succeed in drawing under their authority the archbishopric of Constantinople whose first archbishop was Antony Nouridjian. His authority extended over all Asia Minor, except over the order of Zmmar.

In 1866 Antony Hassoun was called to the see of Constantinople. He was proclaimed patriarch and Pius IX, in 1867 confirmed it by his bull REVERSURUS, giving him the title of Patriarch of Cilicia. Thus the patriarchate of Zmmar was suppressed.

After the Great War, the seat of patriarchate was by the order of the pope transferred to Beirut. Terzian, who was patriarch at the time, died. His successor is Monseignor Avetig Arpiarian, former patriarchal vicar.

Rome contributed much to the success of the Catholic Armenian patriarchate of Beirut and constructed at his expense an establishment for the patriarchate at Eshrefieh.

THE ARMENIAN PROTESTANTS

Beginning in 1838, the Union of Presbyterian Churches sent missionaries to Constantinople and to Smyrna, as well as to the interior of Turkey, in order to propagate protestantism among The Moslems.

But they could not succeed, and carried their activity amidst Armenians. This activity, at first, was marked by a series of good works, such as the publication of the Holy Scriptures in modern Armenian and in Turkish, the latter with Armenian characters, and also the foundation of schools and hospitals.

The population, being plunged in material and intellectual misery, appreciated the services which the American missionaries rendered. The lower classes, poor and unfortunate hastened voluntarily into their schools and their various establishments. The American good works served to entice the Armenians.

The Armenian patriarch of Constantinople, in order to defend his flock protested against the propaganda of the missionaries, as he had done formerly against the catholic missionaries. The Turkish government authorities favorably accepted the protestations of the Armenian patriarch. But, as always, the Turks finished by recognizing officially the Protestant Armenians as a separate community in 1850.

In this way, the activity of American missionaries was legalized, so, they resumed their task with more energy. Constantinople, Smyrna, Aintab, Kharpout, Marzouan, Marash were given colleges, hospitals, mixed schools and theological institutes.

By these means protestantism penetrated and developed in the bosom of the Armenian people.

The protestant Armenians are more numerous than the Armenian Catholics, despite the century-long efforts of Rome.* That is to say, the American missionaries have rendered much more service to the Armenians in one century than the missionaries of Rome, whether Latin or Armenian, have been able to render in several centuries.

●

---

* The number of Catholic and Protestant Armenians does not amount to more than two hundred fifty thousand; that is, 8% of total Armenians.

THE SUPREME HIERARCHY OF THE
ARMENIAN CHURCH
THE CATHOLICOS OF ALL THE ARMENIANS

The ranking person in all ecclesiastical hierarchy, the supreme head of the Church is the patriarch of Etchmiadzin, the Catholicos* of all the Armenians.

The Catholicos of Etchmiadzin divides the supreme jurisdiction of the Church with the patriarchs of Constantinople and of Jerusalem and the Catholicos of Sis, without derogating from the primacy of the see of Etchmiadzin and in hierarchical unity of the Church.

The last three sees are of later origin and were created under the pressure of political and historical conditions in which Armenia and the Armenians found themselves.

The same political conditions necessitated frequently, the moving of the seat of the Catholicos of Etchmiadzin to Dvin, to Ani, to Roumkale, to Sis and again, finally to Etchmiadzin, in 1441.

After the fall of the Bagratid** kingdom, the

---

* The title of Catholicos is given to the Patriarchs of Etchmiadzin and Sis. It means the highest office in the hierarchy.
T. V. P.

** The Bagratids were descended from noble and brave Armenian families. Their dynasty was founded in 859; it played a very important role in the history of the Armenian nation. The first king of the Bagratounian dynasty was Ashod to whom the Caliph Mehmedjafar gave the title of "prince of princes." In 886, the Caliph and emperor Basil I made a treaty of friendship with him. Ashod II "The Iron" and his

Armenians withdrew from before the floods of invasions and transferred their activities beyond the Euphrates, into the territory of Minor Armenia. They succeeded in establishing a new state in Cilicia which lasted until 1375*. On account of these conditions the catholicoses were installed in 1147 in Roumkale, and in 1293 in Sis, until 1441.

The advantage which had attracted the Catholicoses to Cilicia disappeared when the Armenian kingdom of Cilicia collapsed.

An assembly held in Etchmiadzin in 1441 decided to transfer the see from Sis to Etchmiadzin.

---

brother Appas, who succeeded him, were famous for their fortitude and wisdom. Ashod III was the most outstanding figure among the Bagratid kings. He with his Queen Khosrovanoush built magnificent churches, schools, hospitals, monasteries—Sanahin and Haghpad—which became centers of learning. He gave all his personal income to charity, and established alms-houses and state charities. He was called "The Merciful" because of his being so benevolent and so interested in the poor. During the rule of Bagratids 1001 churches were erected in Ani, the capital of the kingdom. The magnificent cathedral of Ani, and the innumerable monuments and irrigation works which were built all over the country, the ruins of which stand out until today exhibit the constructive genius of the Armenian nation.

The Bagratounian dynasty collapsed in 1045, partly on account of constant Byzantine efforts to convert the Armenian Church to Greek orthodoxy, and partly on account of the Seljuk hordes which devastated the Arab and Persian territories and made repeated incursions into Armenia.   T. V. P.

* After the fall of Bagratid Dynasty many Armenians crossed the Taurus Mountains and established an independent kingdom in 1080. The founder was the prince Reupen, a scion of the Bagratid princes.

The Cilician kingdom of Armenians lasted three hundred years. During that period Lesser Armenia flourished in culture, art, literature, and architecture. Sis was the capital of the kingdom where the catholicos established his seat.— The magnificent patriarchal throne was made of white marble; in 1921 it was shattered by barbarous Turks. The Ar-

48

The catholicos Gregory Mouradpekian, who at this time was accupying the throne did not submit to the decision of the assembly and continued to reside at Sis. The assembly elected another catholicos, Giragos of Virab. Thus the patriarchal seat was reinstalled in Etchmiadzin, where it is found until now.

The election of the Catholicos used to take place according to the constitution called Bologenia, published in 1836, and also according to the statute elaborated in 1843 by the Synod of Etchmiadzin and confirmed by the Tzar.

The Catholicos was elected in an assembly com-

---

menian kings and princes became famous for their bravery. They had many dealings with the Crusaders and Mohammedan powers. They made an alliance with the Mongols against the Memluks of Egypt. In 1198, Pope Celestine III sent to King Leon II a decorated crown by the hand of Conrad, Archbishop of Maguntia. The German emperor Henry VI sent him a splendid standard, having in the middle a lion rampant, in allusion to his name.

The success of the Crusaders was due to the Armenian kings of Cilicia, who gave them aid after their terrible march through Asia Minor. Armenians delivered them from the horrors of famine and pestilence, and from the Seljuk invasions. Baldwin got possession of Edessa with the help of the Armenian king.

But unfortunately the Crusades became the chief cause of the downfall of the Cilician kingdom. The Moslem Memluks of Egypt and the Ottoman power on the west destroyed the kingdom of Cilicia because the Armenians were in correspondence and communication with western nations. They imagined that the Armenians were stirring the Western powers against them. Europe despite her promise did not send any help; she left the Armenians to their fate.

The last Armenian king, Leon VI, died in Paris and was buried in St. Denis. The following epitaph, which I read is inscribed on his Tomb:

"Here lies Leon VI, The Noble Lousignan Prince,
The King of Armenia,
Who died 1393 A. D., November 23rd, in Paris."

posed of two kinds of delegates of each eparchy, one ecclesiastic and the other a layman. Two candidates were elected in this Assembly and submitted to the Tzar who confirmed the election of one as the Catholicos.

Attached to the Catholicos there was a Synod whose members were appointed by the Tzar upon the recommendation of the Catholicos. A procurator at this Synod represented the government.

The Armenian Church in Russia comprises six eparchies placed under the authority of Archbishops. Each eparchy has a consistory for regulating the affairs under the presidency of the Archbishop himself.

●

THE CATHOLICOS OF CILICIA

After the split of 1441, Gregory and his successors continued to reside in Sis, and in order not to cause confusion, they took the name "Catholicos of Cilicia". The jurisdiction of the seat of Sis stretched over a vast territory; formerly it included even Jerusalem. Before 1915, it had sixteen dioceses in the boundaries of Adana, of Aleppo, of Sivas, of Angora and of Kharpout. Only the villayet of Adana belonged entirely to the see of Sis; the others were only partly dependent. The island of Cyprus after some waverings between Sis and Jerusalem was placed among the dioceses of Sis.

Until 1871, the catholicossate of Sis became hereditary in a family called Adjbahian. The intervention of the patriarch of Constantinople was necessary to put an end to this monopoly. An assembly composed of the laity and the clergy elected the archbishop of Angora, Meguerditch, a native of Marash, and had his election confirmed by the Sultan.

After the death of Meguerditch which happened on the 8th of November, 1894, it was impossible to elect a successor, and the see remained vacant, occupied by a locum tenens until 1902. The assembly summoned on the 12th of October in Adana elected as Catholicos the Archbishop Sahak, a member of the monastery of Saint James of Jerusalem born on the 25th day of March, 1849, in the village of Eghek near Kharpout.

THE PATRIARCH OF CONSTANTINOPLE

The patriarchate of Constantinople has existed since 1461, at the time when Sultan Mahomet II invited the archbishop of Broussa to transport his see into the new capital of the empire, and granted him the dignity of PATRIK (patriarch) with all the prerogatives that the Greek patriarch had. His official title is "Archbishop of Constantinople, patriarch of Armenians in Turkey".

The jurisdiction of the patriarch included 45 dioceses in Turkey, and the Armenian colonies of Egypt, Bulgaria, Rumania and Greece.

The patriarch of Constantinople took a preponderant place in the administrative organization of the Armenian Church especially after 1860, when the right to administer affairs passed into the hands of the National Assembly. This was composed of deputies elected by public ballot, in compliance with prescriptions of the "National Statute of the Armenians" confirmed by the imperial IRADE and figured, as the law of the state, in the DESTOUR.

The General Assembly is composed of 120 members, clergy and laity, elected by the dioceses. This Assembly elects two councils: RELIGIOUS and CIVIL for the administration o f religious and civil affairs. These two councils together form the Mixed Council, which creates subcouncils or offices to manage educational and judicial affairs.

It is the General Assembly which elects the patriarch.

The election of the patriarch was formerly confirmed by the "ferman" of the Sultan. The patriarch personally presented himself to the Sultan and received the decoration.

The government confirmed the councils.

The patriarch was recognized as an intermediary between the Armenians and the Sultan and his government.

The office of patriarch is not permanent; he can resign voluntarily, or be removed from his office by the vote of the General Assembly in compliance with the dispositions of the statute.

The resigned patriarch is but an ordinary bishop. He can be re-elected.

The General Assembly used to elect prelates for dioceses and the Sultan confirmed them by his edict. The diocesan prelates as such, were the members of the local MEJLIS IDARE (leading council). The prelates were not elected for life; they could be removed from their office or dismissed.

Each diocese elects its own Religious and Civil Councils, that are confirmed by the Patriarch.

●

THE PATRIARCH OF JERUSALEM

The patriarch of Jerusalem for centuries has had the task of guarding in Palestine and chiefly in The Holy City, the special rights of the Armenian Church and also those rights which she shares with the Greek and Roman Churches.

The common rights of the three churches extend over the Church of the Nativity in Bethlehem, the Church of the Resurrection in Jerusalem, and the Church of the Blessed Virgin in Gethsemane. In addition, the patriarch superintends, conjointly with the Greek patriarch, the ruins of the Church of the Ascension on Mount of Olives, where divine service is held two times each year.

The seat of the patriarch is installed in the monastery of Saint James.

The monastery possesses a Seminary, and a valuable library, rich in Armenian manuscripts.

The patriarch of Jerusalem is elected by the General Council of Saint James and in former days was approved by the patriarch of Constantinople and confirmed by the Sultan. His spiritual power extends over Palestine.

After the occupation of Palestine, the English proclaimed the Armenian Patriarchate of Jerusalem independent of that of Constantinople and decided that the election of the patriarch hereafter should be approved by the king of England.

The late Patriarch Yeghishe Tourian, as well as his successor, the present* Patriarch Torkom, were approved by the king of England.

---

* Deceased on February 10, 1939.

THE PRESENT CONDITION

The serious events which took place during and after the Great War have had tragic repercussions on the lot of The Armenians and upset the organization of the Armenian Church.

The Russian empire collapsed, and the Soviet Regime after having decreed the separation of the State from the Church, took a distinctly hostile position toward all religions.

However, the Catholicossate of Etchmiadzin was able to oppose its moral authority against the revolutionary tempest and save at least the dignity of the Armenian Church, with the spirit of tolerance which is characteristic of her through the centuries.

The see of the Catholicos of all the Armenians was stripped of all its possessions by the measures of secularization. Even the library of the Catholicossate was secularized.

The statute called BOLOGENIA was abolished. The synod changed its name to Supreme Spiritual Council. The mode of election of the Catholicos has remained in effect.

It was according to the ancient statute that the General Assembly, composed of laity and clergy of diocesan delegates, raised to the patriarchal throne the locum tenens of the catholicossate Archbishop Khoren Mouradbekian.

The PATRIARCHATE OF CONSTANTINOPLE

suffered a fate as cruel as irrepairable. Its flock was exterminated or deported from its country.

The new governmental system in Turkey declared itself in favor of the separation of Church and the State. On this pretext they stripped the Church of all her properties and of all her instiutions. The secular privileges which she had obtained with difficulty, were abrogated. The educational establishments, so admirably organized, disappeared. She was despoiled of all her possessions which were secularized. The little which remained as rights of a national minority was violated by the government. In brief, all that she had attained under a despotic regime was lost under a "democratic" regime.

Under these conditions the jurisdiction of the patriarchate was reduced to a narrow power in very confined limits. In spite of this the seat of Constantinople has maintained the high prestige and the great respect which she previously used to enjoy among the Armenian people.

The Assembly and the Councils continue to administer the affairs of the Church. The present patriarch, Archbishop Mesrob Naroyan, was elected by he National Assembly, but the government did not confirm him, in virtue of the new constitution of the State.

THE CATHOLICOSSATE OF CILICIA was struck my the same misfortune. The Turkish barbarism shattered the beautiful Armenian Cilicia. Its Armenian population was deported during the Great War. As soon as peace was restored the survivors returned in search of their ruined homes. But hardly had these unfortunate people raised up their houses when a new disaster came upon them and forced them to quit their homes again. This story is well known and too sad for us to repeat it again.

The eminent spiritual head of this unfortunate population Catholicos Sahak, that noble old man, shared with his people all the adversities of deportation and of exile and came finally to look for a place of rest in Syria.

Lebanon particularly was ready to open her gates to a people escaped from their executions.

The patriarchal see of Sis, which was a heritage of the Armenian kingdom of Cilicia, had all that past glory could bequeath her; the moral influence, the material prosperity appropriate to her high position. The unjust fortune which bitterly struck the Armenian people, did not spare the seat of its spiritual head. Catholicos Sahak, bent under the weight of his years took his cross again to accompany his flock toward an uncertain refuge. He found it in Syria, where he breathed freely. The good welcome which the humane population of the country gave to the refugees, the friendliness which the native and French governments showed towrads them proved a true comfort for them after so many misfortunes and sufferings.

The years 1915-1930 were very painful for the refugees who found themselves living almost insurmountable difficulties. But because of their courage and tenacity they emerged from this period of misery.

The Catholicos endured his hardships courageously in spite of his age and situation. General Weygand, the High Commissioner, favorably disposed toward the Catholicos, encouraged him to plan for the organization of the spiritual jurisdiction.

Never did the existence of the see of Cilicia seem so indispensable as now, for the good reason that the two centers of the supreme hierarchy, Etchmiadzin and Constantinople, are limited if not paralyzed in their action.

First of all it was indispensable to secure the necessary means and to call someone to assist the Catholicos because of his advanced age. The see of Jerusalem was the first to facilitate the task of the Caholicos by placing at his disposal some properties which it had in Syria and Lebanon in the cities of Aleppo, Damascus, Laodicea and Beirut. These cities had houses, and shops which had been given to the patriarchate of Jerusalem by pious persons. . . . .

Catholicos Sahak conferred with Yeghishe Tourian, the Patriarch of Jerusalem who consented to yield to the catholicossate not only his possessions but also the diocesan jurisdiction of Jerusalem over Damascus, Beirut and Laodicea.

After the transfer of properties the catholicos moved from Aleppo to Beirut to establish his seat.

Beirut, the capital of the Lebanon Republic and the center of all spiritual jurisdictions was the city best qualified to become the seat of the catholicos. In addition, the High Commissioner was of the same opinion. Fortunately the Catholicos selected Antilias, one of the suburbs of Beirut. The Orphanage of the Near East Relief, which had been constructed for the Armenian orphans and partly by themselves, was then vacant and attracted the attention of the Catholicos, who succeeded, thanks to the beneficence of the Near East Relief, in installing there the seat of the Catholicossate. It was necessary to make some repairs and some changes in order to adjust the buildings to their new use. A church was constructed, a seminary and a press were founded; a monthly magazine, "HASK", the official organ of the see, was published, thus enlivening the see and making it a luminous focus, a center of spiritual and national culture.

The contribution which the Near East Relief and some Armenians in the United States gave, enabled the opening of a Seminary even in the first year, under the direction of Bishop Shahe Kasparian.

If the see succeeded in a short time in completing its physical equipment and in getting to work, it is thanks to the generosity of Mr. Karapet Melkonian. This noble Armenian of Alexandria annually gives a thousand Egyptian gold pounds to provide for the needs of the see and its establishments. We want to point out this fine gesture of the great benefactor Melkonian who by his remarkable generosity has deserved well at the hands of all our people.

After the installation of the see, the organization of dioceses was begun. The regions of great cities, such as Aleppo, Beirut, Damascus, Laodicea and the Isle of Cyprus formed dioceses. Their administration is based on the electoral right, confided to the people. . . . .

Catholicos Sahak, because of his advanced age, did not feel able to finish this work of organization. So, at the very beginning he called to his help Bishop Papken, the former prelate of Angora, and the director of the Armenian Seminary founded by himself in Jerusalem.

The organization being completed, Catholicos Sahak wanted in his lifetime to provide a successor for his seat. He summoned an assembly of the representatives of the people, which approved his resolution and choice. Thus, Bishop Papken was solemnly consecrated Caholicos in the Church of the Forty Martyrs, in Allepo, on 25th of April, 1931.

The see of Cilicia preserves from antiquity, among other relics, the right hand of St. Gregory the Illuminator, which is held in great veneration among the Armenian people. . . . .

●

THE HISTORIC AND
TRUE NAME OF OUR CHURCH

The Church of England means the Church of the English people. In like manner, our church is called THE CHURCH OF ARMENIA, or THE CHURCH OF ARMENIANS, or simply THE ARMENIAN CHURCH.

The bodies separated from the Armenian Church are called:

a) The Armenian (Roman) Catholic Church.

b) The Armenian Protestant Church.

The appellations: Armenian Gregorian Church, Armenian Apostolic Church etc., are wrong.

We want the name ARMENIAN CHURCH to be respected because it is the historical and real name of our church.

THE END

CONTENTS